The Anointing of the Minstrel

Tom Bynum

Unless otherwise indicated, all Scripture quotations were taken from the Holy Bible, King James Version.

The Anointing of the Minstrel
Copyright © 1993 Tom Bynum
Printed in the United States of America
All rights reserved.

ISBN - 1-880324-05-9

New Wine Publications
P.O. Box 6843
Chicago, IL 60680

Dedication

I would like to dedicate this book to my wife, Samantha Bynum, for her sacrifice and support, without which, this book would not have been possible.

Acknowledgements

I would like to acknowledge my publishers and editors, Timothy and Tanya Stokes, who have toiled and labored with me, countless hours. Through all of the last minute changes and troubles, they stuck right with me to the bitter end. Tim and Tanya, thanks for all of the late nights and wee hours of the morning.

I would also like to acknowledge New Wine Christian Center, who have given up so much to allow me to not only complete this project, but be the shepherd God has called me to be.

I would like to acknowledge the minstrels of New Wine Christian Center. Special thanks for their hard work: Gregory Landfair, Jan Hill, John Hill, Malcolm Banks, Keith Jackson, Kenny Davis, Jimmy Cobb, and Alvin Carter.

Last, but not least, I would like to acknowledge Thomas and Katherine Bynum, my precious mom and dad.

Table of Contents

CHAPTER ONE

The Purpose of the Minstrel

In the Twentieth Century, the anointing of the minstrel and psalmist has been the most neglected gift that exists today. The office of the minstrel and the psalmist has been abused, misused, suppressed, and cast aside. Until this day, we have not seen the true manifestations of God's purpose for the minstrel and psalmist.

To my knowledge, the late Jimmy Hendricks was not born again, yet there was something spiritual that happened to him when he played the guitar. He had a call and a gift on his life. He knew he had a unique gift, but he never knew his purpose. You also may be a gifted minstrel or musician, but you do not know your purpose. What God wants to do is thrust you into your purpose.

The difference between a minstrel and a musician is that a minstrel plays from his heart, but a musician plays from his head and is very technical. A musician plays from head knowledge. Therefore, he can only play what he knows. He generally plays things the same way all the time, without deviation. On the other hand, a minstrel is a heart player. Minstrels are spirit-inspired, they play by unction and spontaneity. Although the minstrel has knowledge, he is more unction-led than knowledge-led.

Jimmy Hendricks was the devil's minstrel because he did not play under the inspiration of the Holy Ghost. Minstrels may not be as knowledgeable as others, but they are a step ahead of them because they are spirit-led. Musicians are just led by knowledge.

If you are a musician who is not born again, you are playing beneath your privileges. There are high and low impact musicians, just as with aerobics. Even as a Christian musician, if you do not play for the Lord by your spirit, if you are not led of the Lord in your playing, then you are operating in low impact minstrel activity. You need to learn how to get into the high vein of the spirit of your calling.

You are not playing according to your potential until you play from your spirit, under the inspiration of the Holy Ghost. Even if you have gone to music school or seminary, your education is incomplete until you have learned to play not only by your understanding, but by your spirit. This occurs by being in total submission to the Spirit of the Lord as a minstrel.

I believe that Jimmy's downfall was that his friends worshipped his call and his gift. They did not encourage him to play for the Lord. When they began to worship his call and his uniqueness, it became perverted and distorted. It was used for the devil and not for the kingdom of God.

You may have people around you who worship your call by saying, ''Oh, you are good. You are bad. You have what it takes.'' However, these type of people will never launch you into your purpose. Instead, they usually serve as the greatest hindrance to you flowing in the purpose for which God created you. You need to surround yourself with people who are going to launch you into the height of your calling.

Jimmy Hendricks, who was one of the greatest guitar players of all time, learned to throw himself into music. During one interview, he said that upon walking out on the platform to perform, his spirit left his body.

An African tribe had a ritualistic chant that was identical to one of Jimmy Hendricks' recordings. Jimmy Hendricks had no foreknowledge of the chant, however, they had tapped into the same spirit realm. There are only two spirit realms - one of God and one of evil. That is why it is critical for your spirit man to be yielded to the Spirit of God in order to bring forth His purpose and not the purpose of the devil.

There is a force that a guitar carries. It can fire

into the depths of a man's soul and cause him to react. God wants His anointed minstrels to get under the mantle of David, just like Jimmy Hendricks was under a mantle. I am not saying it was the mantle of God, but he had a call on his life that was distorted and aborted because people worshipped his call.

A mantle is a special endowment. It allows the minstrel to play under the hand of the Lord or by the Spirit of the Lord. However, if it is perverted, he will be led by the devil in his playing. David had the ability to change spiritual climates. He had the ability to play and usher in the presence of God or drive out the presence of evil forces. He operated under the mantle of the Lord. God wants His minstrels today to operate under the same mantle or anointing that David played under.

Jimmy Hendricks was before his time. Musicians, when you are before your time, if you are not careful, a spirit of pride can come upon you as people idolize your gift. Jesus was a man who was before His time. He was casting out devils and the people desired to worship Him. However, Jesus' response was to withdraw from them. He would go into the mountains and wilderness to pray so that He remained in the will of the Father and not His own will.

People seek something or someone whom they can worship. They do not want to worship God, they want to worship things that are tangible, things that are in the sense realm. They want to worship musicians, sounds, and tunes. God wants minstrels to put the focus back on Him and not on how great they are, what school they graduated from, what band they used to play for, or who has the best choir and organist. He wants the minstrels to redirect the praise back to Him so that He can use them to set the captives free.

If you are a minstrel, I just want to loose you into another realm. There is a higher call and realm that God is wooing and beckoning you to enter. It is possible for you to enter into that realm. It is a glorious realm. God wants to take you to a place in the spirit that will turn on the prophet's anointing to prophesy more. He wants to take you to a place that will ignite the anointing of the psalmist, so that more songs of the Lord will be written. Remember, God created music for His pleasure.

The minstrels in the house of God today need to be loosed. Sometimes pastors bind the musicians in the house of God, by limiting them to express themselves through certain sounds. We need to give minstrels space in the house of God, so they can begin to play from their spirits in response to unction and not just rehearsed songs.

The Bible says that there are different kinds of music (Ecc. 2:8). The Church needs all kinds of music and sounds. It is going to take different sounds to usher in different anointings, administrations, and operations of the Spirit of God. You may wonder what that has to do with church. It has a lot to do with church.

I believe, in the Twentieth Century, we need all sorts of musical instruments in our worship services.

We need the flute players, the guitar players, the horn players, and the bass players. We also need men who are anointed on the organ, as well as those who are anointed to blow the trumpet in Zion and sound the alarm on the holy mountain. This will allow the people of God to enter into deeper realms of the spirit and receive from God, because God is a Spirit.

By the truths shared in this book, it is my endeavor to launch you to a higher realm and a higher call in the spirit. The Bible says there are different administrations and different operations of God, but it is the same Spirit (I Corinthians 12). You may have never seen certain operations of the Spirit musically. However, there are many things that God is doing that you have never seen. You must be willing to humble yourself before Him and say, ''God, if this is what you want to do, if this is how you want to do it, I am here to receive from you.''

Release your gift unto God and let Him express Himself through you. This will cause you to enter into the depth of your calling. It is in the spirit of humility, whereby the Holy Spirit will lead and guide you into the truth concerning your purpose.

CHAPTER TWO

DeliveranceThrough the Minstrel's Office

There is a way for a minstrel to play under the unction of the Holy Ghost that will bring healing and deliverance to the heart of man. When certain chords and sounds are anointed, they drive out evil forces. We know this is true, by examining the life of King Saul.

> *But the spirit of the LORD departed from Saul, and an evil spirit from the LORD troubled him.*

> *And Saul's servants said unto him, Behold now, an evil spirit from God troubleth thee.*

Let our lord now command thy servants, which are before thee, to seek out a man, who is a cunning player on an harp: and it shall come to pass, when the evil spirit from God is upon thee, that he shall play with his hand, and thou shalt be well.

And Saul said unto his servants, Provide me now a man that can play well, and bring him to me.

Then answered one of the servants, and said, Behold, I have seen a son of Jesse the Bethlehemite, that is cunning in playing, and a mighty valiant man, and a man of war, and prudent in matters, and a comely person, and the LORD is with him.

Wherefore Saul sent messengers unto Jesse, and said, Send me David thy son, which is with the sheep.

And Jesse took an ass laden with bread, and a bottle of wine, and a kid, and sent them by David his son unto Saul.

And David came to Saul, and stood before him: and he loved him greatly; and he became his armourbearer.

And Saul sent to Jesse, saying, Let David, I pray thee, stand before me; for he hath found favour in my sight.

And it came to pass, when the evil spirit from God was upon Saul, that David took an harp,

and played with his hand: so Saul was re-
freshed, and was well, and the evil spirit
departed from him.

I Samuel 16:14-23

People can be set free just from the power of a
skillful minstrel. No one called a prayer line or laid
hands on Saul, nor did they throw a bucket of olive oil
on him. He just called for David, who was an anointed
minstrel, to play the instrument. As he played, the evil
spirit left Saul.

There are different sounds that are in the spirit
and every sound touches a different part of a man's
emotions and his soul. That is the power of music - it
is the power to a man's soul. Music, chords and
melodies can go into areas of the soulish realm where
some preaching and words cannot penetrate.

The devil has a counterfeit for anything that
God has established. He has deceived the Church into
believing that every other sound is of the world if it
doesn't come out of Dr. Watt's hymnal. There are
sounds in the spirit that can judge the heart and soul of
a man. They can penetrate the heart, crack open the
chains of bondage and set him free.

Right now, God's power is flowing upon the
hands of musicians. God is anointing musicians to play
under the unction of the Holy Ghost as never before.
He is raising up high impact minstrels! God is raising
up men and women who understand how to play under
the unction of the Holy Spirit to set the captives free.

In one particular service that I was conducting, the Lord told me, "Tom, there are people here who have emotional pain, emotional breakdowns." In response to that word from the Lord, He instructed me to call for a guitar player. As I called him up, I told the people to line up across the front of the altar. I then asked the guitar player to begin playing.

A pastor must understand that the musician may not always know what you want, but you have to instruct him as to what you want. The guitar player didn't know where he was going in the spirit. This was all new to him, but I was working with him letting him know what I wanted as I began to sound out the notes with my mouth.

What we have in services today is a pastor who will say, "Play something," and then say, "That isn't it, play something else." Sometimes, if the man of God can just hear something in his spirit, he can vocalize it in order to bring the musician to a place where he can come as close as possible to what he desires.

There is something that the world has tapped into musically. The Bible says the children of this world are in their generation wiser than the children of light. The world has successfully used music and instruments as a net to capture society, while the Church has suppressed music and thrown it out of services as if to say, "All we need is preaching."

I had the guitarist stand directly in front of those people who were suffering from emotional pain, and play. As he began to play, people began to weep.

They began to cry and fall under the power of God. This was a form of deliverance. Saul was vexed by devils and he didn't know how to get free. The Bible says that Saul called for David. As David began to play upon the harp (there is a Hebrew word for praise that is called Zamar, which means "to strike the strings"), the evil spirits left Saul and he was a free man.

Music - The Power to Your Soul

People of God, the world has tapped into music's power in the soulish realm and this is what the Church has suppressed and neglected. Utilizing music's power is called a different administration and operation of the Spirit. You may not be used to seeing it, but I believe the days are coming when the prophet will point to the drummer and say "play" and the drummer will play until people get healed, set free, and delivered. I also believe that the days are coming when the guitar player will begin to play and those chords will hit the soul of man and bring deliverance. There is deliverance in music.

In another instance, something began to happen when Saul, who was a stubborn man, was walking into a city where the minstrels were playing tabrets and the psalmists were singing. God was attempting to get Saul's attention. The Bible says the Spirit of the Lord came upon Saul, knocked him down and changed his heart. God replaced his stony heart with a soft heart. Saul even began to prophesy with the prophets.

Psalmists and minstrels create an atmosphere for an individual's life to be changed. In the life of the late Jimmy Hendricks, we have witnessed the power that minstrels possess in setting a certain atmosphere. Music and minstrels set the climate or atmosphere in any environment. Again, it can be used for good or for evil. The world understands the power of music and the song, but the Church doesn't.

I believe music takes a man out of his spirit. It causes a man to go into another place. When Jimmy Hendricks would play, his spirit would go into another realm or another place. He reported that his spirit would not even be there, he would just be playing. Was this satanic? Of course it was because he was not entering into the spirit under the inspiration of the Holy Ghost for the kingdom's sake. However, that confirms music's power and ability to allow one to escape from one realm into another.

What makes a woman in the audience, when a man begins to play the guitar, take off her underwear and throw them on the stage? What makes a woman take off her clothes during a concert? What makes a woman pull her hair and scream, ''Play it! Play it! Play it!''? It is because that particular form of music has tapped into a part of her emotions and soul that has never been penetrated.

There is an excitement that comes with certain

sounds and depths of music that takes people out of themselves. It causes them to behave out of character. Music has the ability to take a person out of character. What God wants to do, my friend, is bring you out of character - that old, stale, dry character of gloom, defeat and depression.

God wants to raise up minstrels so that when they begin to play, it will touch people where words cannot go, it will heal the wounds and bind up the brokenhearted.

The world is stealing the hearts of men by way of music. We know this is true because when people get saved, the hardest thing for them to release is their music. If the world has that kind of impact musically, then the music in the house of God must be strong! It will have to posses depth. It must have spiritual force! By this I mean, our musicians are going to have to play until they are infused by the Holy Ghost.

There are realms in the spirit that we have not tapped into. Jimmy Hendricks was a man who tapped into the spirit world. God is raising up minstrels who will tap into His world. There is a whole realm that God wants His minstrels to reach where they will release new wine and fresh oil into the people of God.

Jimmy Hendricks was one of the greatest guitar players that ever lived. He was always consumed with the music he played. God wants you to have a similar experience, except you won't be tapping into evil spirits, but into the realm of the Holy Spirit. He wants you to pull the goodies down that are in the spirit realm and release them in the natural, so that His people can be set free and changed. It is time for the minstrel and psalmist to arise! Arise in the house of the Lord!

There are people who are bound in their spirits and souls and they don't know how to get free. In many instances, they have been preached to and counseled for years, seemingly everything that could possibly be done has been done. These people need a breakthrough in the spirit. The only way that their breakthrough is going to come is through the assistance of an anointed minstrel. They need someone who has a minstrel's anointing on them to begin to play until devils leave! Play until devils cry! Play until they are set free from the enemy's oppression!

People will begin to break under the power of the Holy Ghost and the power that comes through the anointing of the minstrel. That is why you must understand that the minstrels must be loosed in the house of the Lord. They must have the freedom to allow the creativeness of the Father to manifest.

CHAPTER THREE

The Skill of the Minstrel

There was a testimony that came from one of my recent services of a young lady who had emotional ties with a man from a former relationship. This had caused a great deal of inward pain.

In this particular service, the Lord told me that the spirit of David was in the house. I called up a guitar player and I gave him instructions as to how to play. The Lord told me that there were sounds in the spirit that had strength and power! Sounds that were as strong as the sounds that you would probably hear in rock music.

There were people in the audience who had a problem with the screeching, screaming sound of the guitar. But they didn't have a solution for this young lady's dilemma. That is the biggest problem in the Church; people open their big mouths, full of entirely nothing, but pessimistic, dogmatic, religious hogwash.

You must remember that the Apostle Paul said that the manifestations of the Spirit are so that we may profit withal. A church will never profit or reap spiritual benefits if they do not allow the manifestations of the Spirit to operate. They will be NON-PROFIT organizations spiritually and legally. You can argue with the administrations of the Spirit, but you cannot deny the manifestations or results.

As I was saying, the sounds that came forth from the instrument were sounds of strength and war. As the minstrel began to extract or pull violent, forceful sounds out of the spirit, these sounds began to penetrate the depths of her soul. In Proverbs, 3:20, it says, ''By his knowledge, the depths are broken up and the clouds drop down the dew.'' The Bible also says my people are destroyed for lack of knowledge. The lack of skillfulness in a minstrel will limit his ability to set others free. The more skill and knowledge that a minstrel possesses, the greater his ability to usher in the presence of God and to cause the oppressed to be loosed.

You must understand that music and love songs can be used to bring a closeness and create a soul tie or a bonding in a male/female relationship. If it can be used to facilitate the tying of souls, then it also can be used to undue the tying. In the case of this young lady, she needed the soul tie broken. That is exactly what God did, using the skill of the minstrel.

Praise the LORD with harp: sing unto him with the psaltery and an instrument of ten strings.

Sing unto him a new song; play skilfully with a loud noise.

Psalms 33:2,3

As I mentioned before in the first chapter, a minstrel must learn to play from his spirit. Psalm 33:2 says, ''Praise the Lord with harp,'' which means that a minstrel should learn how to use his instrument as a tool to worship God. Notice, in verse three, it says, ''Sing unto him a new song.'' Then it also says, ''Play skillfully with a loud noise.'' Notice that the bringing forth of the new song or the song of the Lord is mentioned in the same text as ''play skillfully with a loud noise.''

There should be a very close relationship between the psalmist and the minstrel and between the prophet and the minstrel. When the psalmist brings forth the song of the Lord, verse three says, that the minstrel should play skillfully. In other words, the skillful minstrel will enhance the song of the Lord. When a minstrel is skilled, he has the ability to use certain chord progressions and bridges. This skill will enable the psalmist to not only bring forth the song of the Lord, but to literally compose a song on the spot.

The majority of the songs that we sing in our

local church are original songs that came forth out of my spirit as I brought forth the song of the Lord.

You must remember, there is the creation of the song or the bringing forth of the song, then there is the perfecting of a song. In other words, when the song of the Lord comes forth in a service, perhaps it is just two lines or just the chorus. The ideal thing to do is to allow the Holy Spirit, at a later time, to build around the song and add verses and bridges that will bring about the completion of the song.

The Prophetic Song

And he divided the three hundred men into three companies, and he put a trumpet in every man's hand, with empty pitchers, and lamps within the pitchers.

And he said unto them, Look on me and do likewise: and, behold, when I come to the outside of the camp, it shall be that, as I do, so shall you do.

Judges 7:16-17

Paul says, follow me even as I follow Christ. If you are going to flow prophetically, you will have to learn to focus on the leader and follow him.

What is prophecy? Prophecy is a series of inspired words placed in your spirit. Likewise, the prophetic song is a series of divine or inspired words put to melody. A rebellious or unsubmissive minstrel will never learn to flow in the prophetic, because the prophetic is under God's leadership. The prophetic minstrel and psalmist must always be under leadership. God wants to teach you how to flow in the prophetic song. When you are flowing in the prophetic song, sometimes God uses different flows and different types of music. Flowing in the prophetic song is very simple. The minstrel helps the psalmist to tap into that vein. The psalmist are arising!

"Something new is happening!!!!!!!"

A different sound is coming. God is changing the sound. If you want to be in on it, dive into it!!!!!!

The entire book of the Song of Solomon was sung. The song of Solomon was called the song of songs. Solomon tapped into a prophetic flow and could not come out so he just sang the entire book of the Song of Solomon.

There is deliverance in singing unto the Lord. There is divine power released from heaven if we learn to use the song of the Lord in times of battle. Gideon learned to use the song of the Lord in times of battle and so should you. People of God, you need to get into a place where worship is strong and the anointing of the minstrel can come forth ushering in signs and wonders.

Tips for a Successful Minstrel

Preaching and music are one. Music is not over

here and preaching over there. When the word of the Lord comes forth and music comes forth, it is to function as one. When the man of God begins to preach with music behind him, it aids him in the spirit. As a minstrel, you need to be so flexible. Minstrels should never have to be asked to play. That minstrel should be seated at the keyboard in that church service through the entire service ready to assist the pastor.

The pastor may get up and read a scripture and say, ''Lift your hands and say, 'praise Him.''' Some pastors preach in that vein. We have charismatic, calm, sedate teachers, then there are those who just preach and they need the assistance of minstrels.

When the minstrels back up the preachers on the instruments, the word of the Lord comes forth with power and strength and it blasts over the audience. If the minstrel steps out of service to get a drink of water, and never returns because he is fellowshipping with other musicians, then he will be out of the flow of the service. While he is in the hallway talking, the preacher continues to deliver the word of the Lord.

At the conclusion of the preacher's message when he calls for a musician, the musician gets on the keyboard and starts to play something totally contrary to the spirit of the word that was preached. This happens too often in service. However, if he were in the service and if the preacher was in a preaching vein, when he gets to the keyboard he knows that the music he plays needs to be strong and aggressive.

If the musician was sitting in the service and the

preacher just finished preaching on the blood. It is not warfare, it should not be played in a minor key. Most warfare music is played in minor keys. He is preaching on the blood, now he wants to make an altar call. The musician would then play something worshipful that speaks of the blood of Jesus. There are different kinds of music that have different effects on the souls of men.

When the minstrel begins to play soft music while the preacher is talking, his message goes uninhibited. However, if you have a nine piece band, then all nine pieces should not be playing, you should only here one instrument, the piano or the organ. Sometimes if a man of God is talking it sounds too junky behind him. It sounds like a jazz band playing. There is too much commotion because the musicians are drowning out each other.

When one instrument is playing, then his voice is heard accurately. The music is then setting the atmosphere while the man of God is ministering the word of the Lord. That is how a minstrel should flow in a service.

When the preacher calls for a healing line, I have found that minstrels should not play something soft and molotic, unless there is a special anointing for that style of music. When you play slow music, sometimes the minister takes more time praying for people, people react slower, everything is slower. If you are in a healing line and you begin to play something that has a beat to it, it keeps that charge and anointing in the building when that ministry gift is laying hands on people. He can then lay hands on people in the rhythm of the music. The music in the house of the Lord needs to be so fine tuned in the hour in which we live.

> *Also the Levites which were the singers, all of them of Asaph, of a heman, of Jeduthun, with their sons and their brethren, being arrayed in white linen, having cymbals and psalteries and harps, stood at the east end of the altar, and with them an hundred and twenty priests sounding with trumpets:)*

> *It came even to pass, as the trumpetors and singers were as one, to make one sound to be heard in praising and thanking the Lord; and when they lifted up their voice with the trumpets and cymbals and instruments of musick, and praised the Lord, saying, For he is good; for his mercy endureth for ever: that then the house was filled with a cloud, even the house of the Lord;*

> *So that the priests could not stand to minister by reason of the cloud: for the glory of the Lord had filled the house of God.*

II Chronicles 5:12-14

The Levites were the preachers and they were minstrels as well. They were on the cymbals, psaltries, harps, they stood at the east end of the altar and with them a hundred and twenty with trumpets.

Notice, in verse thirteen, that all the music was as one. In other words, John Doe was not just doing his own thing on the drums. The key board player didn't have his eyes closed as if he were in his own world, neither did the guitar player. It should not be that way.

The minstrel's eyes should be glued to that ministry gift at all times. The musicians should be as one. They should make one sound. They should be unified. In other words, there should be sound checks. There is nothing more disgusting than a musician coming in late, setting up at the last minute when he should have been there for a sound check.

We need to understand that the minstrel's office and anointing will aid and assist the preacher. It will directly affect, in a positive or negative way, the anointing or climate that is in that service. It will also affect the attitude of the people. Music is just that powerful.

Another tip for a successful minstrel would be that a minstrel should NEVER take it upon himself to play repetitive, chordular, phrasing when accompanying a psalmist or preacher, unless otherwise asked by the psalmist or preacher. If this is done, it could lock the psalmist into repetitive phrasing. For example, with the old familiar song, ''Praise Him:''

Praise Him, praise Him
Praise Him in the morning
Praise Him in the noonday
Praise Him, praise Him
Praise Him when the son goes down

If the repetitive, chordular phrasing is played during the last phrase of this song, *"Praise Him when the son goes down,"* then this will lock the psalmist into this particular song. It will inhibit the psalmist from flowing into another song or medley. He will be locked into singing the same phrase, *"Praise Him when the son goes down, Praise Him when the son goes down, Praise Him when the son goes down."*

You see, it would make it very difficult for him to come out of the song, unless he completely ended the song. Sometimes, if that happens, that could slow down the momentum of the worship service. You must remember that you are not participating in a song service, but you are coming into the throne room of God to worship Him.

Another tip for the minstrel, is when psalmists are singing minstrels should always play in such a manner that the words of the song are heard and fully understood. When the psalmist is singing, the music should be lower than the voice to accompany the song of the Lord.

When the bridge or interlude is played, the minstrel can enhance a song with crescendo and accents during the interlude and de-crescendo at the completion of the interlude so that the voices can again be heard. This will enhance and increase the dynamics of the song, sometimes - notice I said, ''sometimes.'' If you attempt this all the time or if you add too many accents, then the music or the song will become too busy. The song will sound like ''Worthy is the Jam!'' instead of ''Worthy is the Lamb.'' Remember, the Lamb is always worthy!

God loves the minstrel. Notice when Elisha prophesied, he called for the minstrel. The Bible says as the minstrel played, the hand of the Lord came upon Elisha. If nothing else will move the hand of God, the minstrel possesses the innate ability to do it, every time.

The Characteristics of a Minstrel

> *Then answered one of the servants, and said, Behold, I have seen a son of Jesse the Bethlehemite, that is cunning in playing, and a mighty valiant man, and a man of war, and prudent in matters, and a comely person, and the LORD is with him.*

I Samuel 16:18

During the time when Saul was vexed by evil spirits, he and all of his kingdom sought for someone who could alleviate the spiritual unrest in his life.

According to I Samuel, chapter sixteen, verse eighteen, notice that they said that they knew a man who was cunning in playing. The first characteristic of a minstrel is that he must be cunning. You must understand that this word cunning is taking from a Hebrew word "Yada," which means perceptive, observant, caring, and of great recognition. This word also means intimacy, one that is skillful and have great knowledge of animals, hunting, lamentation, and sailing the sea.

You may be asking the question, "What does the knowledge of animals have to do with playing? What does the knowledge of hunting have to do with playing? What does the knowledge of lamentation have to do with playing? What does the knowledge of sailing the sea have to do with playing? What does the knowledge of being observant have to do with playing? What does caring have to do with playing? What does perception have to do with playing? What does recognition have to do with playing? What does intimacy have to do with playing?

Notice, that verse eighteen says that David was cunning in playing. Everything we've just listed, is descriptive of the Hebrew word, "cunning." Let's look at the word perceptive as it relates to David's playing. Every minstrel must be perceptive. You must know when to play aggressive music and when to play soft music. You must know when to play sounds of war and when to play sounds of worship.

Let's look at the knowledge of animals. David

tied the knowledge of animals into his playing. As David, the shepherd, he would use a different approach to destroy a lion, than he would a bear.

As David, the hunter, he would use different approaches to ensnare and entrap different animals. In this he was cunning. He perceived what spirit was on Saul. Then, by playing, he became a predator in the spirit. He tracked down that spirit that was upon Saul, ensnared it, and detroyed it. When David went after that spirit, it was as if he was on a hunt.

Let's look at lamentation. The word lamentation means to be poetic. You must ask yourself the question, "What does a poet do?" A poet paints a picture. In other words, when David began to play, his playing literally painted a picture. It gave Saul a vision of something other than his present dilemma. It literally transported him out of his current state of confusion and took his focus off of his current surroundings.

The minstrel should be so trained, skilled, and disciplined until when the prophet prophesies, "I hear the sound of rain," the minstrel should be able to create the sensation of rain. If the prophet prophesies, "The winds of change have come," then the minstrel should be able to emulate the sound of wind with his instrument.

If the prophet prophesies and start speaking in oriental tongues, then the minstrel should become so poetic in his playing until he duplicates oriental music. That is why it is very important for minstrels to listen and study not only different sounds, but music of different cultures so that they are not limited in their ability to interpret the mood of the Spirit.

Again, the Bible says that the children of this world in their generation are wiser than the children of light. We can see what is taking place now in the earth. You have the devil's minstrels putting together subliminal tapes of sounds, winds, and waves. These tapes are literally being used to accomplish the same purpose. I am telling you, the devil is a counterfeit!

Let's look at the sailing of the sea. The cunningness is in how the sailor adjusts the sail to capture the momentum of the wind and propel the vessel to its destination. Likewise, David would tap into the spirit, capture the anointing, and it literally thrust him, as the vessel of God, to the place of deliverance.

Let's look at the word observant. David, as a minstrel , was observant. A minstrel should always be observant. An example of this, in a church setting, a minstrel should never have to be asked to come to his instrument. If a minstrel is observant during a church service, then he would sense when the minister is concluding his message. He would then automatically get to his instrument, which means a minstrel should always remain inside the service.

If a minstrel is not in a service during the message, he really does not know what is being taught. The speaker could be ministering in a strong warfare vein in the spirit and if the minstrel is not in the service. If the minstrel is not in the service, when he gets up to accompany the speaker, he would play something contrary to the current flow of the ministry gift.

David was caring. He had the ability to touch. He knew when, where, and how!

Recognition is also a meaning for the word cunning. In other words, David was recognized as a minstrel and psalmist because of his skill and confidence concerning his call.

The word intimacy also comes from the word cunning. This means that David was intimate in his playing. In Hebrew, it is recorded that David was intimate in playing as one who is intimate with his wife. This means that he was not just acquainted with playing, he had the ability to release the expressions of his spirit through the instrument, as if it were a part of his very own body and he became one flesh with it. In other words, when David played you could literally feel the impact of every note! It penetrated the heart, mind, and emotions of man.

> *Then answered one of the servants, and said, Behold, I have seen a son of Jesse the Bethlehemite, that is **cunning in playing, and a mighty valiant man, and a man of war, and prudent in matters, and a comely person, and the LORD is with him.***

I Samuel 16:18

The second characteristic of the minstrel is that

he must be a mighty, valiant man. David was forcefully courageous. He had punch in the spirit. When he played his instrument, he was aggressive.

The third characteristic of a minstrel is that he must be a man of war. David was a man of war. He not only knew how to express the compassion of the Lord from his instrument, but also militancy.

The fourth characteristic of the minstrel is prudence. David was prudent, which means to be wise in matters.

The fifth characteristic is a comely person. A minstrel should be a person with divine favor.

The sixth characteristic of the minstrel is that the Lord is with him. The sign of a true minstrel of God is that the Lord is with him.

CHAPTER FOUR

Appointed and Anointed

And God hath set some in the church, first apostles, secondarily prophets, thirdly teachers, after that miracles, then gifts of healings, helps, governments, diversities of tongues.

I Corinthians 12:28

God set some in the church, Apostles, secondarily prophets, thirdly teachers, evangelists, and pastors. This means that everyone cannot function in the office of a prophet or apostle, because He only gave "some" that responsibility. Even if you prophesy, that does not mean that you are a prophet. Paul said, I would that ye all prophesy. However, that has no bearing on the foundational gifts that God has set in the church.

And these are they whom David set over the service of song in the house of the Lord, after that the ark had rest.

And they ministered before the dwelling place of the tabernacle of the congregation with singing, until Solomon had built the house of the Lord in Jerusalem: and then they waited on their office according to their order.

I Chronicles 6:31,32

Just as with the foundational gifts that were set in the church, notice that the singers did not volunteer to minister, but David set these people over the service. You may wonder, ''Why doesn't he pick me, I have a good voice?'' God is not concerned with your good voice. He has specific people whom He desires to use to get a certain job done.

Don't get upset if God is holding you in His quiver right now. God is just hanging on to you and grooming you. Don't get upset if the man of God does not point you out and say, ''I want you to do this. Come along and travel with me.''

Don't get upset or dismayed - do not despise your day of grooming. This is how people's ministries get shipwrecked. They go off on their own prematurely because they despised their day of grooming and the small things. God has a time and a season for you. In your time and season God is going to raise you up, anoint you, and put His mantle on you. There is a process that you must go through in order to receive God's mantle. He will first call you, then appoint you and anoint you for His service.

In the Old Testament, they set singers in the church, just as God set gifts in the church. They were very selective in who they allowed to sing and play instruments.

The Bible says that they called for the ''skilled'' musicians. Again, the anointing of the minstrel includes being skillful. He must understand how to play a traditional sound, a charismatic sound, a melodic sound, a worship sound or a Pentecostal dance sound. You need to be well-rounded. The more well-rounded you are, the more you give the Holy Ghost to work with. The Holy Spirit may want to use a certain sound to break up and destroy different yokes.

Remember, there are different administrations and operations of the Spirit. If we will learn that, we will not be bound. We would submit to the Holy Ghost, allowing Him to operate through us as He desires and when He desires. It is through submission to the Holy Ghost that our souls are liberated.

The force of a minstrel's office will come from him spending time with the Lord. In order for a minstrel to usher the people into the presence of the Lord, he must first be able to usher himself into God's presence.

If a musician cannot usher himself into God's

presence, then he cannot take the people of God into the presence of the Lord. If what you are playing doesn't inspire you to worship, it will not inspire others.

The first thing a minstrel needs to do is wait quietly in God's presence and still his spirit so that he can properly receive the sound for the occasion. Every service is different and every service has a different focus. If a minstrel will wait quietly in God's presence he can receive insight and direction from the Lord.

But they that wait upon the Lord shall renew their strength; they shall mount up with wings as eagle; they shall run and not be weary, and they shall walk and not faint.

Isaiah 40:31

In other words, when a minstrel spends time waiting in God's presence he renews his strength. Strength is the Hebrew word ''Koach.'' That word literally means ability, force, fruit, might, power, substance, and wealth.

The word renew in the Hebrew means to stretch or exchange. This means that if a minstrel spends time waiting in God's presence then he renews, or stretches, or exchanges his weakness or limitations for God's. In actuality, if a minstrel is limited in knowledge, sometimes by waiting in God's presence, it will make up the difference (remember I said ''sometimes''). Most minstrels because of their lack of education concerning music, they are prone to feel inferior. But remember, when you surround yourself with minstrels who are stronger than you, it will only enhance your ability to pull down God's power.

Notice that Isaiah 40:31 says, they that wait upon the Lord shall renew their strength. I recently discovered that the word strength in the Hebrew, also means ''numbers.'' This means that when a minstrel waits in God's presence, he will have the ability to duplicate himself. The anointing that is on his life will increase and multiply.

CHAPTER FIVE

Playing Under Authority

Of the sons of Asaph, Zacur, Joseph, Nethaniah, and Asarelah, the sons of Asaph under the hands of Asaph, which prophesied according to the order of the king.

Of Jeduthun: the sons of Jeduthun; Gedaliah, and Zeri, and Jeshaiah, Hashabiah, and Mattithiah, six, under the hands of their father Jeduthun, who prophesied with a harp, to give thanks and to praise the LORD.

I Chronicles 25:2,3

They prophesied according to the order of the king. In other words, the king would be talking and he would point to the minstrels and they would begin to play under the order of the king. This is key.

Notice how the minstrels were under the hands of Jeduthun. He was telling them what to do and they obeyed. The reason the service that I ministered at with the guitar player was anointed, with the power of God present to set the captives free, was because I instructed the musician and he played under my hand or authority.

There were six musicians under the hands of their Father, Jeduthun. The Bible says that the spirit of the prophet is subject to the prophet. God will not give anything to a prophet that he will not give to the psalmist or minstrel. So, I believe that the spirit of the psalmist is subject to the psalmist and the spirit of the minstrel is subject to the minstrel. Therefore, musicians must be very careful not to enter into pride. In other words, your spirit man is subject to you. Your gift is subject to you.

If you are a musician, you are not called to operate independently in the house of the Lord. You are not called to set your own program or agenda. You cannot arrive late for service, practice when you want to practice, and play when you want to play. That is prideful. You are in the army of God. It is vital that you learn your place and position in the church, which is God's kingdom.

You may be a minstrel and say, ''Well, I just can't play like that. I just don't like that flavor or that taste of music.'' Who cares! God is trying to get a specific work done and He needs you. God wants to use bass guitar players, organ players, lead guitar players, horn players, and saxophone players. He needs you to be under the hands of authority and not stroll in church late making excuses in an attempt to justify his tardiness.

In the Old Testament minstrels arrived to service on time. They arrived even hours prior to the service of the Lord. Today, there are musicians who arrive late to service, yet they want to be paid. You need to be kicked out - that is what some of you need.

Musicians must be punctual. If you are a minstrel, you need to arrive at service early enough to hear what the Spirit of the Lord is saying to the church. The Old Testament minstrels were under the hand of their father who prophesied with the harp to give thanks and to praise the Lord. God wants to bring you to a place where you are punctual and operating under the hand or authority of your leadership.

There must be a pastor - psalmist relationship, and a pastor - minstrel relationship. Pastors must tell the minstrels and psalmist what they need in order to orchestrate the move of the Spirit in each service. If a minstrel is not skilled, he will bind the hands of the psalmist, henceforth, the psalmist will bind the hands of the prophet. The Bible says that when Elisha began to prophesy, he called for the minstrel, and as the minstrel played the hand of the Lord came upon Elisha.

Often, we just want to rely on song sheets. Thank God for song sheets, but the days are at hand when the minstrels will have to learn to be under the hand of the prophet and the pastor. That is called being prophetic - inspired by the Spirit of God to address the current needs in that service.

I Chronicles 9:33, says the minstrels were set in the house of the Lord and that they were on salary. I believe some musicians need to be staffed. The minstrel is as important as the preacher. However, if the ministry is pressed for finances, the minstrel shouldn't have an arrogant attitude whereby he cannot play unless he's paid. That attitude is carnal, ungodly and of the devil. If you have that attitude, you are a hireling. You need to ask yourself, ''Am I a hireling or do I work for the Lord?'' The Bible says, ''Go into the vineyard and work; and whatever is right, I will pay.''

Prophesying on the Instruments

''Moreover David and the captains of the host separated to the service of the sons of Asaph and of Heman and of Jeduthun, who should prophesy with harps, with the psalteries, and with cymbals: and the number of the workmen according to their service was.''

I Chronicles 25:1

The musicians were given for song. They prophesied upon the instruments. This is coming back into the kingdom. We will begin to see people prophesy on instruments.

You may be a musician who is called of God, but unless you are prophesying on that instrument, you are playing below your privileges. Some people live beneath their privileges, likewise, you are playing beneath your privileges. You are in the arena of low impact ministry. You need to get into that high vein where you begin to play under the unction and from your spirit. Begin to play what you hear and allow the Holy Ghost to lead you into all things. God wants you in that place where you begin to flow.

Notice that the minstrels prophesied with the psaltry, harp and with cymbals. Drummers are going to begin to prophesy. In a recent service, God had me call out a gentlemen. Now remember, I had no knowledge of his profession. I called him to the platform. I instructed all the minstrels and musicians to stop playing. This was in a visiting church, and the drummer didn't have a clue as to what I was doing and where I was going.

I instructed him to play unto the Lord. I gave him an example, with my mouth, of what I wanted him to do. There was total silence throughout the entire church. The drums were the only instrument playing at that time. I began to speak prophetically to the gentleman that I had called from the audience. I told him, ''The devil has totally destroyed your whole life.''

As I began to prophesy to him, I told him that the power of God was going to invade the enemy's turf and beat upon the foundations of the devil's kingdom. At that moment, I instructed the drummer to start playing. I told him that I didn't want a beat, but I wanted him to play as if he were playing a solo on the drums.

As he began to play, I told the gentleman that I was prophesying to, that the sound that I heard in the spirit was a sound of God doing great damage to the enemy's kingdom. I heard, ''crash, bang, pow. Crash, bang, pow.'' I told the drummer to duplicate those sounds on the drums.

When that began to happen, the gentlemen that I was prophesying to broke and began to cry. Before I could touch him, he hit the floor like a ton of bricks, weeping and crying. The Spirit of God set him totally free.

Later, I was informed that this gentleman was a professional drummer. I know that it sounds strange to most religious people, but again God can do what He wants to do with music. You can't put a big God into a 3 x 5 mind.

A minstrel should be ready, at all times, to play prophetically. Minstrels need to know that they should flow prophetically on the keyboard, just like the minstrels who were under the hand of Jeduthun. They flowed accurately in the prophetic.

I have put my keyboard player in some very tight spots. At the close of one sermon I told him to put my message in a song. The Spirit of the Lord came upon him to play prophetically as I had requested of him.

When David wrote he always said, "'to the chief musician.'' Whenever he preached, decreed a law, or spoke the oracles of the Lord he said, "Give this to the chief musician'' and the chief musician would put it in a song.

I asked my chief musician what takes place in his spirit when I spontaneously make a demand on his gift.

He responded, I would listen to you and enjoy the message, as I received from God. It puts me on the spot when you would request, 'Keith, put that in a song.' I would then pray, 'God I need your help now.' Then I just tuned in, played and sung as God gave me the words. It comes from a relationship of praising and worshipping Him.''

Keith said that God will show Himself faithful to a musician who spends his time worshipping Him, giving Him the glory, telling Him how much he loves and cares for Him, and not playing just by skill. Keith arrives about two hours before each service begins, worshipping God and just playing before the Lord in order to hear what He would say to the church musically that day.

And these are the singers, chief of the fathers of the Levites, who remaining in the chambers were free: for they were employed in that work day and night.

I Chronicles 9:33

And Chenaniah, chief of the Levites was for song: he instructed about the song, because he was skillful.

I Chronicles 15:22

There were musicians whose job was to sit in the house of God and play. They began to sing over and around the ark of the Lord. Keith also does this before service. I asked him, "What vein does that put you in when you get a chance to spend time playing before the Lord?"

His response was, "When I come to church and worship God, I feel an unction. I love to be in the presence of the Father. I love to be in the sanctuary just worshipping God, when no one is there. During those times, I am able to minister to God and He is able to minister to me. There is a love relationship going on. This time prepares me for the praise and worship service. It liberates me. I may have had difficult situations in my life, but when I come and minister to the Lord, He is able to minister to me and free me. He heals my wounds."

Every minstrel needs to have a very close relationship with the Lord. They need to remain in constant fellowship with the Spirit of God in order to enter into the depth of their calling.

CHAPTER SIX

Beware
of
Perversion

Musicians, there are certain spirits that want to bring you down, hinder and stop your flow. That is where being under the hand of authority provides a covering, just as David was under the authority of King Saul.

And David went out whithersoever Saul sent him, and behaved himself wisely: and Saul set him over the men of war, and he was accepted in the sight of all the people, and also in the sight of Saul's servants.

I Samuel 18:5

If you are going to be set in position in the church as a minstrel, you have to learn how to behave wisely. Understand that David went out whithersoever Saul sent him. If you are a minstrel, you need to be able to play and assist the man of God in whatever realm he flows in. Being under authority will break the power of the enemy in his attempt to pervert you, your gift and your calling. You will render worship unto the Father in a spirit of purity, therefore, allowing the Holy Spirit to flow through you and anoint you for His purpose.

There are certain spirits that dog the trails of each musician. The spirit that dogs a bass player's trail is laziness. Bass players, a lot of times, like to be in the background. Most bass players are quiet. Although they would prefer being in the background, God is going to bring them to the forefront. God will cause the boldness and courage to come. In the days to come, a mighty roar and thunder will be sounded from the office of the bass player.

Musicians, you need to understand that just because people praise you and describe you as being great, it is not your show. It is God's show. You still need to be under authority. When you are under authority, it causes the anointing and the power to flow much more accurately and at a deeper dimension.

There are some musicians who will become perverted if they are not careful. Perversion is something every minstrel has to battle. The word perverse means "crooked." You have to battle with being crooked. Lucifer was beautiful. He never said, "Move over, let me play the Hammond B3 organ;'' he was the Hammond B3 organ. He was made out of music. He was made to glorify God, but he became haughty and said, ''I will exalt myself above the throne of God.'' Satan is still attempting to receive glory and that is why he has such a stronghold on the music industry - minstrels and psalmist.

Again, I have found that there are certain spirits that follow certain musicians. One of the pitfalls of guitar players is that they can be sucked into the world. They have a strong spirit of the world to contend with. Spirits of the world are always pulling at guitar players because the world knows the power of a guitar.

Drummers must be careful with whoremongering. You have to be careful of the whoremonger spirit that can get on the drummer and that can cause you not to keep your dress down or your pants zipped. If a minstrel is not careful, he will cause all kinds of ungodly and devilish spirits to be released in the house of the Lord by transference of spirits. That means, if a minstrel plays out of a spirit of perversion then that spirit can be released throughout the body.

Like bass players, horn players have strong lazy streaks. You have to be careful, horn players, that you don't get lazy in the house of God, that you don't just drag your feet concerning the things of God.

Key board players, a lot of times, battle with the spirits of homosexuality. Minstrels must remain spiritual. An unspiritual minstrel will grieve a psalmist. An unspiritual psalmist will grieve a prophet. An unspiritual prophet will grieve the church because it will hinder him from flowing in accurate operations. Consecration will strengthen and sharpen the flow.

You must remember that Lucifer was the chief musician in heaven. When he tried to exalt himself above the throne of God, he was kicked out of heaven.

The word "perverted" means, "crooked." The reason spirits of perversion attack the psalmist and minstrel office is because Psalm 49:4 says, "I will incline mine ear to a parable: I will open my dark sayings upon the harp."

You must understand that a dark saying is a hidden saying. God said that He would open His dark sayings upon the harp. That means, hidden revelational truths and spiritual illumination can be unlocked and revealed by the power of the minstrel. That is why the devil wants to pervert them. If the minstrel is perverted, he cannot unlock those revelational truths.

The book of Psalms was not preached, but sung and so was a great portion of the Old Testament. It takes the anointing of the minstrel to tap into the full meaning and revelation of these books. If it took the minstrel to release the revelation then, it will also take this same anointing to unlock the secret to the revelation now. Thus, Satan seeks to pervert all minstrels and psalmist to prevent the disclosure of the dark sayings of God and keep the church dimly lit.

How can a minstrel guard against being perverted? A minstrel must have consecration, the right association, and surround himself with minstrels

who are spiritually stronger to receive proper imparta-
tions. A minstrel must not be in denial of his character
weaknesses. The Bible says that iron sharpeneth iron.
If he will stay in the right fellowship, then God will
send the proper spiritual reinforcement as a source of
strength to him. This was evident in the case of
Jonathan being a source of strength for David.

CHAPTER SEVEN

The Ministry of Helps

If you don't understand the ministry of helps, you will never understand the purpose of the minstrel, psalmist, or the new song. You must understand that the anointing of the minstrel and psalmist is not a one-man show. It is not the choir, preacher, worship leader, key boardist or drummer operating independently of one another.

God wants to teach us to flow and to tap in to the spirit corporately. Helps is a spiritual operation and administration. In the nineties, there are certain realms in the spirit that you will never reach unless you learn the operations of true spiritual helps.

If you don't think you need help, just ask that old, dead, dry Hammond B3 you have been banging on for years. If you don't think you need help, ask your choir and worship leader.

Every worship team leader and member, every psalmist, every quartet, every choir, every prophet, every apostle, and every church needs the ministry of spiritual helps operating and functioning in their lives. If our ministries are going to grow, flourish and be the beacon light God is raising up in these last days, then He wants to teach us how to flow in spiritual helps. God has set some in the church first, apostles, secondarily prophets, thirdly teachers, after that miracles, then gifts of healings and then helps. There are certain realms you will never tap into unless you first learn the administrations of spiritual helps.

And Elisha said, As the Lord of hosts liveth, before whom I stand, surely were it not that I regard the presence of Jehoshaphat the king of Judah, I would not look toward thee, nor see thee.

But now bring me a minstrel. And it came to pass, when the minstrel played, that the hand of the Lord came upon him.

And he said, Thus saith the Lord, Make this valley full of ditches.

II Kings 3:14-16

Here is a story of three kings who were wandering in the wilderness. They were wondering where they would get water from and whether they would even survive. Three men were calling for Elisha the prophet. They thought, ''We know that Elisha can hear from God because he was the one who poured water on Elijah's hands.'' They called for Elisha, but he didn't want to help them. Elisha did not care what they needed or wanted. He told them to go to their own prophets and leaders in their own land for direction. these three kings were in the desert, they didn't have water and were in desperate need of it so they called for Elisha.

Elisha did not want to service these men, but he called for a minstrel. When they brought the musician unto him, the Bible says it came to pass when the minstrel played that the hand of the Lord came upon him and he began to prophesy. It wasn't until the minstrel began to play that the hand of the Lord came upon Elisha.

Musicians have the innate ability to cause the hand of the Lord to come upon a man of God. As they play, it releases things from another realm. If the man of God has the right music working with him it will push him beyond his limitations, even if he does not feel like preaching or prophesying. That is called spiritual helps. It will cause him to be propelled and launched into another realm. He will prophesy like he has never prophesied before. He will preach like a man from another world.

The anointing of the minstrel and psalmist can literally take a man of God out of character. It can make him become so spiritually minded, so heavenly minded that he can get more information from heaven for your good in one service than you could possibly conjure up in all of your long hours of prayer.

When the minstrel played, the hand of the Lord came upon Elisha. If you want the hand of the Lord to come upon you and rest in your services, sometimes you have to release the minstrels to play.

Again, Elisha was a man who didn't want to prophesy. He didn't feel like prophesying or preaching. However, when the minstrel played, the hand of the Lord came upon him and he said, "thus saith the Lord..." This is why I like music playing when I am prophesying. I like the right music playing because it puts me in the right realm so that I can impart unto people every single thing that God has released unto me in a particular service.

For thus saith the Lord, Ye shall not see wind, neither shall ye see rain; yet that valley shall be filled with water, that ye may drink, both ye, and your cattle, and your beasts.

And this is but a light thing in the sight of the Lord: he will deliver the Moabites also into your hand.

II Kings 3:17-18

The Lord released the whole battle plan not

because of the prophet, but because the minstrel functioned in the ministry of spiritual helps. He helped the prophet get to another realm in the spirit.

If I were to preach to you, you would get a cassette tape of that message and listen to it approximately 3 or 4 times. However, if I gave you a music tape, you would listen to that song repeatedly. This is the power of music. It is so important that even when the prophet began to prophesy, he called for a minstrel.

Minstrels, you should function with the prophet, pastor, or shepherd that is ministering. That is why knowing a variety of sounds is so important. When the man of God begins to prophesy and say, ''I am the God of the rain.'' I believe there should be a synthesizer that would have the sound effects of rain. If he says, ''I am the God that moves upon the waters,'' there should be a sound played by the minstrel that demonstrates moving upon the water. If the man of God is prophesying and he is saying, ''I shall be with you in the quiet times.'' The minstrel should demonstrate the quiet times.

If the prophet continues, ''And in the quiet times, I shall bring strength to you. For yes, I am the all sufficient God. I am the God of might. I am the God of power.'' The minstrel should become more dramatic in demonstration of the prophetic word of the Lord. That is how a minstrel can flow with a prophet as he is prophesying. It aids the prophetic voice. It gives a punch!

The people will never forget that experience.

They will never forget when God said, "I am the God
of might." Not only did the word of the Lord hit them,
but the music was there. It adds impact to the word of
the Lord! These are things that you need to understand.
If you would tap into that realm, you will find out that
the prophet would prophesy with more revelation and
accuracy. When the minstrel begins to come forth by
playing behind the prophet or ministry gift by respond-
ing to his promptings, it aids a man in preaching.

If we are going to get anywhere in the 90's, God
wants to cause the office of psalmist and minstrel to be
elevated. For too long these ministry gifts have been
suppressed. You may not think that degree of music
flowing in the church is necessary. You would just as
soon have a white haired old lady playing on a Hammond
B3 organ. Your attitude may be, "Away with the
synthesizers, away with different sound effects, leave
that in the world, you are bringing the world into the
church." However, when people cannot remember the
word of the Lord through a preached message, they can
remember a song. The song of the Lord is important.
Prophetic singing is important.

> *Then Samuel took a vial of oil, and poured it
> upon his head, and kissed him, and said, Is it
> not because the Lord hath anointed thee to be
> captain over his inheritance?*
>
> *When thou are departed from me to day, then
> thou shalt find two men by Rachel's sepulchre*

in the border of benjamin at Zelzah; and they will say unto thee The asses which thou wentest to seek are found: and, lo, thy father hath left the care of the asses, and sorroweth for you, saying, What shall I do for my son?

Then shalt thou go on forward from thence, and thou shalt come to the plain of tabor, and there shall meet thee three men going up to God to Bethel, one carrying three kids, and another carrying three loaves of bread, and another carrying a bottle of wine.

And they will salute thee, and give thee two loaves of bread; which thou shalt receive of their hands.

After that thou shalt come to the hill of God, where is the garrison of the Philistines: and it shall come to pass, when thou art come thither to the city, that thou shalt meet a company of prophets coming down from the high place with a psaltery, and a tabret, and a pipe, and a harp, before them; and they shall prophesy:

And the Spirit of the Lord will come upon thee, and thou shalt prophesy with them, and shall be turned into another man.

I Samuel 10:1-6

Minstrels were assisting the prophets. He was talking to Saul. Saul was hard-headed, stubborn, and walking out of the will of God. However, the Spirit of the Lord still came upon him as the minstrels played. Saul was a guy who did not prophesy. He wasn't even considering prophesying. However, the hand of the Lord came upon him also because the minstrels were playing and the prophets were prophesying. Some of you have the ability to minister.

It is not because you are so anointed, or so grand. It is only because the church that you are connected with allows you to prophesy with the prophets and the minstrels, causing you to be turned into another man. Now that you have changed, you are flowing in a vein that is abnormal to you. You may think it is because of your greatness or your fasting and praying, but it is not. It is only because of your association with the right atmosphere.

The missing ingredient in the church is the anointing of the minstrel. What is a minstrel? A minstrel is an anointed musician who is called to play skillfully and to change the spiritual climate or atmosphere. Minstrels have the ability to change the atmosphere and that can be positive or negative. If a man of God can get into the right atmosphere, it will cause him to flow beyond his limitations. This is what God is trying to teach us.

The Minstrel's Helpers

For these Levites, the four chief porters, were in their set office, and were over the chambers and treasuries of the house of God.

And they lodged round about the house of God, because the charge was upon them, and the opening thereof every morning pertained to them.

And certain of them had the charge of the ministering vessels, that they should bring them in and out by tale.

Some of them also were appointed to oversee the vessels and all the instruments of the sanctuary, and the fine flour, and the wine, and the oil, and the frankincense, and the spices.

I Chronicles 9:26-29

Notice, that verse twenty eight says that certain of them had charge of ministering vessels. It was their responsibility to set up the instruments and tear them down. Some of them were appointed to oversee the vessels. Could this be the reason why in our local church, that the instruments are broken, banged up, and tampered with? This is because the local church takes lightly the responsibility of the porter.

There needs to be people assigned to oversee and maintain the musical instruments and sound equipment. There also needs to be consistent sound checks to prevent sound distortions during a service. In secular concerts, you will never hear a sound distortion in any given concert. In our local church services, we also need to take the necessary measures to ensure sound quality.

CHAPTER EIGHT

Understanding the Times

If you are a musician, your style, mannerisms and spiritual place in God is about to change. God is changing you because the times and seasons are changing. God wants you to be flexible with the times and seasons.

Ecclesiastes says that there is a time and season for everything and for every purpose under the sun. Not only is there a time and season for a special emphasis to be placed on certain messages, but there are also times and seasons where God begins to use certain instruments and minstrels in a specific way. For instance, there are times when the anointing comes on a guitar player and we have to understand when God wants to highlight the guitar.

During the 60's and 70's, God highlighted the Hammond B3 organ. When the 80's hit, God began to do some things with the synthesizer and special music. The percussion player and guitar will be highlighted in the 90's.

During A.A. Allen's time (40's - 60's), he was an anointed man of God. He knew how to change the climate of the service. I believe that music was the strength of his healing ministry. He knew how to go into a dead, dry setting and change the music, therefore, creating the right environment for healing. R. W. Shambach, who is a dynamic preacher, teacher, and father in the spirit was with A.A. Allen during that time as his announcer/armorbearer/song leader.

A.A. Allen understood the power of music. He understood how to get the people in a spiritual place to receive that which God had for them. He knew how to set the right atmosphere by using the power of music. He was also a minstrel. He played the keyboard, which is very important.

Like many ministry gifts, I am not a musician. However, there are a couple of songs that I can play. If I don't have a musician, I know how to put myself in a vein where I need to be for the Spirit of the Lord to come upon me.

There needs to be a relationship between the prophet and the minstrel, like there was relationship between Elijah and the minstrel. The Bible says when he got ready to prophesy that he called for the minstrel and as the minstrel played, the hand of the Lord came upon him.

Preachers, you need to understand the power of music. You need to understand how to change the climate or atmosphere in your services.

Different music types and styles could bring in

different anointings. There is certain music that musicians can play which causes the prophetic to be very strong in a service. Other songs that they play inspire the word of knowledge. Yet, there are other sounds that ushers in a spirit of might into the service. It brings in the miraculous - miracles, signs and wonders, and aggression in the service.

In A.A. Allen's evangelistic services, they set the climate so that the people would be caught up in the realm of the spirit. This is the power of a minstrel. Minstrels must understand that there is power in music. If we can set the atmosphere in a service utilizing the proper music, it will usher in the power and demonstration of the Holy Ghost.

Again, the children of this world have learned the power of music. In a grocery store, they play xylophone music. While they are playing that music, you are tossing things into your grocery cart to the beat of the music. You have forgotten about your list. You get to the counter and they say, ''That will be $300.'' All of a sudden your eye brows go up, you lose your breath, you go into cardiac arrest and say, ''Three hundred dollars.'' You are spending all of your money because the music was right. It created an atmosphere for spending.

In a men's clothing store, they do not play a lot of sedate music. They play cool music that has a strong beat - it makes you feel cool. You try on an outfit and you are just moving in the mirror. You think you look good. You think that you can someday become a professional model, when actually you can't.

Why do they play that kind of music? To loosen you up and make you feel cool. Then the salesman says, "That outfit is you. You need to buy it in red, white, black, and navy blue." Before you know it, you have spent all your money in the store because the music put you in a groove, until that made you feel good.

When the music makes you feel cool, of course you do not want to dress like you just came from a second hand shop. When the music makes you feel cool, you want to dress cool, you want to pay the cool prices. That is the power of music.

I used to sell Mercedes. When I sold Mercedes, they used to tell me, "Tom, don't play Rock and Roll when you are taking a customer for a test drive in a Mercedes. Don't play rap or jazz." They advised me to play classical music because it made the people feel like caviar and fine wine. It made them feel like the elite. They felt expensive because they were driving an expensive car, therefore, classical music, such as Bach, was more appropriate to set that atmosphere for spending.

When you are getting into an elevator, you hear elevator music - of course they don't want you to hear those cables popping and snapping all the way to the fortieth floor. They play that style of music so that you will just stand in the elevator whistling and patting your feet. The music relaxes you so that you will not become nervous of the fact that you are high up in the air and could fall at any moment. That is the power of music.

You would not want to be in the prep room of a hospital, right before major surgery, and all of a sudden you hear on the P.A. the song, ''Another One Bites the Dust.'' You probably have never seen a wedding or funeral without music. Music is very important in the house of the Lord.

There needs to be a current day relationship between the prophet and the minstrel like there was between Elisha and the minstrel. The church must learn that the reason we have not entered into the realms of the spirit that God has predestined for us is because we have adapted to musical prejudices. If it is not the major gospel chord structure, many people can't get in agreement with certain styles of music. The devil is not the originator and creator of anything. If he can rock 'em to hell, then we can rock 'em to heaven! If he can rap 'em into gang violence, then we can rap 'em into spiritual violence!

True Minstrels Mobilize the Church

And the LORD spake unto Moses, saying,

Make thee two trumpets of silver; of a whole piece shalt thou make them: that thou mayest use them for the calling of the assembly, and for the journeying of the camps.

And when they shall blow with them, all the assembly shall assemble themselves to thee at the door of the tabernacle of the congregation.

Numbers 10:1-3

When ye blow an alarm the second time, then the camps that lie on the south side shall take their journey: they shall blow an alarm for their journeys.

And if ye go to war in your land against the enemy that oppresseth you, then ye shall blow an alarm with the trumpets; and ye shall be remembered before the LORD your God, and ye shall be saved from your enemies.

Also in the day of your gladness, and in your solemn days, and in the beginnings of your months, ye shall blow with the trumpets over your burnt offerings, and over the sacrifices of your peace offerings; that they may be to you for a memorial before your God: I <am> the LORD your God.

Numbers 10:6,9-10

Notice in verse two one of the main purposes of the minstrel's anointing is to call together the assembly. That means to bring the body to the same spiritual wave length. In addition, the minstrels were used for the journeying of the camps.

For a church to grow from faith to faith, glory to glory, and victory to victory the minstrel must take his rightful place. A church's revelation will never exceed its music.

When you come up against spirits that are trying to suppress you in your land, city, or local community you must blow the trumpet, according to Numbers 10:9. The devil has strategically used the seduction of music because he has come to steal, kill and destroy. Likewise, Jesus shall strategically use the power of music to give us life and that more abundantly.

Now I charge you, as a minstrel of the Lord, not to live or play one more day in neutral! I charge you to shift into overdrive!

Other books by Tom Bynum:

The Ministry Gift Error
The Spirit of the Reformer
The Purpose and Operation of Rebuke

For further information or tapes write:

New Wine Christian Center
P.O. Box 6843
Chicago, IL 60680

Nikki

8790958

Monday